Now & Then

Poems of Memory and Reflection

MARTYN POTTS

CP
THE CHOIR PRESS

First published in the United Kingdom in 2020 by
The Choir Press

ISBN 978-1-78963-151-7

Dedication

For Em, Will and Haz

Contents

Introduction

I was born in Blackpool in August 1950. My mum and dad, born in Blackpool and Cockermouth respectively were Fred and Eileen. They met at The Winter Gardens just before the war, not long before Fred was due to leave his homeland for the first time in his life with the 8th Army heading for North Africa.

They married in 1946 not having seen each other for seven years.

We moved to Padiham, then Lancaster and finally the Wirral all to do with Fred's job with the CEGB. He was an electrician who via night school eventually made his way to lower middle-management. Mum worked for Littlewoods Football Pools in Birkenhead near the ferry terminal.

My elder sister Jackie and I were the first in our family to go to university, she in London, me in Manchester. Social mobility, eh! We both became teachers enjoying lives that were in material terms more secure than our parents with foreign holidays that Fred and Eileen could never afford to do with us kids and much more disposable income. They had one foreign holiday revisiting the Italy that Fred had seen during the war. He died aged fifty-six, but Eileen managed to see a lot of the world in her later years.

There is no doubt that my children and countless other young adults of today do not and will not enjoy the same degree of financial security as their parents. Student debt, the gig economy, austerity as a political tool have put paid to the kind of mobility that enabled many, if not all of my generation to live more comfortable lives that their predecessors. If the poems focus on some of this stuff, it's not because I set out to be political, it simply reflects the reality of Now and Then. I may have fond early memories of my early life, but I am nevertheless aware that many coastal resorts and former mill towns are currently experiencing levels of deprivation and poverty that don't match my childhood recollections.

I've been writing poetry of a sort since my early days of teaching when I used to produce a poem for each class I taught at the end of the school year to highlight the books we had read together and to point out the quirks of various class characters.

Pupils seemed to like them so I began to do a staff version for the end of year review including a parody of Under Milkwood for our Dylan Thomas loving Welsh Head Teacher.

Next came birthday poems for family and friends with an odd wedding or anniversary adding to the mix.

Having finished full-time working it seemed right to spend a bit more time and to think more widely about writing. The notion of childhood or teenage life as opposed to life now emerged as I began to write more and since I've lived in the North West all my life it was natural that places and ideas were grounded in this region.

Some of the poems have serious intent as the ageing process leads inevitably to both reflections on mortality and a heightened awareness of the individual lifespan and what it contains.

I started to read the essays of Michel de Montaigne, the 16th Century French writer who was probably the first thinker to look inwards at himself rather than outwards to the external world and to understand the importance of this – our one and only life (unless you believe in reincarnation – all views welcome) rather than some notion of an afterlife which had been the focus for most thought before Montaigne. He inspired me to write about my life.

Perhaps the middle stage of our modern lives with the focus on work, family, busyness and sheer survival is too full on to allow for reflection. Grown up children and no full-time job creates some space that could be filled with all kinds of activities – for me it's writing.

Some of the poems are trivial snippets of memory or observations that occur while walking the dog. Some might even be funny.

The hope is that by sharing these poems some people might recognise the situations, feelings or experiences as similar to their own.

I enjoyed writing them, which is enough in itself.

Bucket and spade list

Sam lived next door
He was older than me
He had a red pedal-car
I didn't
In fact I could just about walk
Never mind sit in a red tin car
Can yearning be a first memory?
I certainly think so
My bucket and spade list
Contained one item
Sit in red car
Propel it forward
With chubby legs
Miraculously it came to pass
Desires have not been met
So easily since then

Padiham

The one-legged war veteran from
up the road used to give us bags of sweets
because they were still rationed.
It was his way of helping local kids
(to keep up their number of fillings?)

We just thought he was a kind old man who liked children.
He would move haltingly towards us with his wooden crutch
Offering gifts, one trouser leg pinned up where the limb was missing.
Did it ever occur to us to ask how he lost his leg?
I don't think so.

Once, a neighbor gave me an enormous orange
that was so big when I put it in the pocket
of my shorts that I couldn't ride my trike.

The mill-shop sold cloth and thread which mum
would buy to make summer shorts and even a
pair of dapper dungarees that once worn I refused to take off.

The toilet was in the back-yard and in winter
nobody wanted to venture outside in the cold dark.

Turf Moor was up the road, a mill-town team
competing with the more glitzy United and Spurs
in a way that would seem impossible now.
Harry Potts was the manager and Bob Lord
The local butcher was the autocratic chairman
Treating players like feudal serfs.

Memories can romanticise, exaggerate or simply fade
But these seem real as ever to me.
We moved elsewhere but the hills and moorland
Still beckon and the stone terraces remain.

Pressing business

There weren't many books in our house
When mum died we sifted and sorted
Pausing to glance at tiny monochrome
Photos with crinkled edges like posh chips
In one heavy old cookery book the pages
Opened to reveal a delicate primrose drained
Almost completely of colour but stilled in time
For more than fifty years since it had been picked
At Silverdale Gibraltar or Arnside on a family
Summer picnic sarnies and flasks stuffed into
The Morris Eight grandma in the front passenger
Seat and us with mum in the back
We had chosen bluebells forget-me-not
Campion and primroses for pressing
To use in making cards for birthdays and greetings
The cookery book's imprisoned bloom
Slipping from the pages like a long lost memory
Reappearing out of time

Butlins

Is it possible to imagine that a week
At Butlins Pwllheli might seem like
The height of sophisticated luxury?
Perhaps in 1956 before Hi-di-hi had
Recreated those thrilling days
With its on-screen version of
Joy hilarity and post-war optimism

Accommodation was roughly on a par
With the average prison cell a bed and
Bunks for the kids a sink but no loo
Or shower – what even was a shower?
I'd never experienced one

Oh, the delight of the washing blocks
Like Stalag whatever but noisier
We loved it

The canteen catered for thousands
Meat and two veg accompanied by
A compere who spun a huge wheel on
The wall to reveal which family had
Won today's bottle of Pomagne
It so happened we had so we stood
On our chairs whilst two thousand
Voices cheered as we sipped from
Plastic flutes and grinned uneasily
At the envious faces around us

Evening variety shows for parents
While teenage Redcoats patrolled
The Chalets in between snogging
Each other in order to baby-sit the kids
Kept everybody happy whilst we were
Exhausted from the day's activities
Races with prizes obstacle courses
Knobbly knees contests and most
Glamorous grannies much fun centred on
The pool where Redcoats buzzed around
Like friendly bees contriving ever more
Obscure ways to push someone into the water
All good fun and no safety concerns
The war had been unsafe so how could
Peace be other than glorious.?

Hacked off

My dad complained that his hacksaw
would not cut through butter
I remembered Dennis the Menace's
answer to a similar enquiry (it was okay
when I sawed a brick in half yesterday)
I on the other hand had been at the tip
with my trolley-building mates*
for several hours cutting through the
drive-shaft of a wrecked car to retrieve
the magnificent steering wheel for the last
piece in the jigsaw that was our Ford
Thunderbird trolley
a bike chain and cog linkage made a crude
somewhat ineffective but spectacular looking
mechanism for guiding our vehicle
rear fins with painted flames nailed onto an
attached box lino covered platform for
up to three seated precariously or lying one
top of the other …
what could possible go wrong
after extensive trials that must have lasted all
of five minutes we set off down the nearest hill
we had neglected to incorporate a braking
mechanism a thought which simultaneously
occurred to the three of us as we hurtled
past the chippy the newsagent's and the
local butcher's with bloody red carcasses of various
dead animals whizzing past in our peripheral

*cart/soap-box depending onwhere you live

vision shoe and sandal leather and in one case
welly rubber wearing at a rapid rate
as our feet sought to slow us down
bodily safety was not our concern but anxiety
that the week-long effort of scrounging wood
raiding the tip purloining tools to put
our creation on the road could be
wrecked in an instant
we hit a wall at an angle front pram wheels
askew all three of us thrown off scrapes
and bruises all over but glory be the
thunderbird held up and was straightened
out and soon equipped with a sort of brake
cum stick-in the-wheel-spokes effort

it was our top activity for all of two weeks
that glorious summer

The Lion and the Lamb

Before motorways existed we often
took the A6 north to the lakes wending
our way slowly through familiar
landscapes making slow progress
in the black Morris 8 rain often
slanting across us from the slate
grey sky that mirrored the fells

to break up the journey in the
pre-digital age we were asked
to spot certain landmarks as
we headed ever northwards
the never-ending-corner
the smallest house in the world and
best of all the Lion and the Lamb
a rock formation perched high up
on the ridge above Dunmail Raise
miraculously on the return journey
it became the Old Man and the Organ
viewed from a different angle

often I was travel-sick in that rattle-box
of a car but even if about to throw up
I would pause mid-heave rather than
miss the sight of what seemed like
such a mysterious natural sculpture

many years later hiking with friends
we came across the very rocks barely
recognisable from a few yards away

proximity does not always reveal
the true picture

Bottle collecting

Leather footballs with a lace to seal
them up like neat sutures on a gash
soaked up water like a sponge despite
the layers of oily dubbin that had to
be rubbed in at regular intervals
I headed a wet ball once in a match
and felt concussed for days it was
some years before I tried it again
 'yours!' becoming a
familiar shout of mine
the first plastic ball was made by
Frido and seemed like a miracle
it didn't knock you out if you headed
it or break your foot when attempting
a blaster from the edge of the box
we played with one on our cinder
covered cul-de-sac until it popped
the flat head of a six-inch nail could
be heated in the coal fire and delicately
applied to the puncture with a surgeon's
touch to melt some plastic over the hole
but a Frido didn't last long after the
first repair and cinders formed a
very unforgiving surface
we found ourselves without a ball
so one entrepreneurial lad (of course
we didn't know what it meant)
had the idea of going round the
cul-de-sac asking for empty pop
bottles to take back to the shop and

claim multiple deposits
after two days some of which was
spent desperately encouraging
families to increase their rate of
pop consumption we had enough for
a new ball a precious collectively
owned ball which required in-depth
discussions in order to decide who
kept it overnight
Billy James got the nod as he had his
own bedroom and could guarantee the
the ball's security from meddling
family members
it was the most cherished ball ever
and by some miracle outlasted
all the others

DIY Capitalism

The James family next door was the first on
Our street to get a television on which
I watched grainy images of Jim Laker
Taking 19 wickets at Old Trafford,
Having been ceremoniously invited in to
Watch with my Dad.
They were also the first to own a Monoply set.
My sister and I spent a rainy half-term afternoon
Being impressed by the glamorous London names,
But the little figures were the best.
Who wouldn't like a tiny, metal top-hat?

We decided to make our own set as
The rainy half-term continued.
Old Christmas cards cut up and the backs
Coloured in for properties.
I sawed a block of wood into dozens of
Houses and hotels, painstakingly
Painting each one, then we voted,
After lengthy boardroom discussions
To go one step further and have
Factories which were brown and
Cost twice as much as hotels.

Not content with Community Chest and
Chance rewards or sanctions we invented
Our own: 'Kid up the road nicks your bike –
You lose £20'
'You find a lost treasure map and discover
Gold worth £2000'
'Dog shits in your footie boots – lose £5
For new Stanley Matthews signature lace-ups.'
We increased the 'Pass Go' salary to £500.
In our world we printed our own money.

Our counters were buttons from Mum's tin,
One shaped like a Scottie dog and one of
A ship's anchor from an old reefer jacket.

Not sure we got the hang of capitalism,
But it kept us out of our Mum's hair
For the rest of the week.
When she died, I found a shoe-box
Under her stairs full of tattered cards
And tiny, misshapen green houses.

Sour Milk Ghyll

A picnic out by Buttermere, with relatives en masse,
With tea and pop and sandwiches set out upon the grass.
The aunties dressed in summer frocks with no intent to walk,
The cousins splashing by the lake, the menfolk sit and talk.

Then Uncle Joe pipes up to say, 'Who's wi' me up yon hill?'
Well soon be up on't craggy path that runs by Sour Milk Ghyll.'
'I'll come,' says I, all nine years old without a worldly care,
With shorts and sandals on my feet and energy to spare.

A carpenter by trade was Joe, he walked the fells for fun,
He didn't slow the pace for me despite the burning sun.
We climbed and climbed, the lake grew small, the top reached
    by and by,
Below us now the gleaming lake, above us only sky.

We came down fast the bilberry stains upon my shorts, but still,
From that day on I loved the fells and know I always will.

The Ginnel

A narrow, fenced-in strip dividing semis from estate,
A path of aspiration to a non-existent gate,
Delineating different worlds, to join or separate.
At ten years old in baggy shorts, two-wheeler bikes in tow,
We stop to see some teenage boys and suddenly we know,
The exit's blocked. They'd have to move to let us through to go.

If we were adults, they would shift, reluctantly, at first,
They wouldn't pick a grown-up fight because they'd come off
     worse.
Round our way, shipyard-working men would take no lip from
     them,
The rules were clearly understood: these lads were not yet men.
We turn around and set off back to ride a longer way,
A mile further round the block, but still we had all day.

I don't suppose it bothered us, our parents unaware,
It's just the way the world was run. It didn't seem unfair.

Quo Vadis?

We were going to the cinema in Birkenhead
Our cousins from Essex were staying and we
Had been allowed go on the bus without
Adult accompaniment a rare treat
The Essoldo was splendidly luxurious
What palaces they were then
Gateways to a magic world of glamour
And endless adventure
The grand foyer the thick carpet and
Best of all, the twin curving staircases
Leading to the upper balconies
We approached the ticket booth the
Girls in their best frocks and me in a newly
Knitted sweater and Sunday- School shoes
Only to discover that we needed to have an
Adult with us because two of us were not old enough
Suddenly the manager appeared in immaculate
Suit with white shirt and bowtie and we thought
This is it we'll be thrown out he'll tell us off
Waiting for the inevitable 'Where do you think you're going?'
We were visibly upset the older girls consumed
By embarrassment and us two youngsters
Feeling guilty because our age was the problem
He smiled and said he'd be the adult for us
So up the grand staircase he escorted us
Until we were in our comfy seats on the first row
Of the grand balcony looking down at all those below
Such kindness was not too common where kids were
Concerned and the incident stayed with me

A few years later in a Latin lesson at school
I finally understood what the title of the film meant
A few years after that I also got irony
Peter Ustinov as Nero fiddling while Rome burned
Chariots and soldiers and epic battles

My favourite childhood film ...
... daft title.

Storeton Woods

Triceratops-like sandstone runs along the Wirral's twisting spine,
With ancient woodland dotted here and there.
Quarries, long since filled, held fossilised footprints, some now
    museum bound,
That we as children clambered up flakey slopes to find.

We walked or scrambled (as we called it) on makeshift bikes,
All second hand, riding wooded paths that meandered through,
Looking for rope-swings or spots for dens in which,
To be buccaneers or cowboys or no-good villains.

I walk there now, some fifty-odd years hence and see
Only dog-walkers with excited cockapoos or labradoodles,
Made to measure pets with names like 'Bruno' or 'Chloe.'
Adults taking exercise for their healthy hearts.

Kids? They are, at best, in malls or private lessons,
At worst, in front of glowing, magic screens, growing fat.

Weapons of past destruction

'the child is father to the man' Wordsworth

If Wordsworth's words have any truth
I should by now be a ruthless
international mercenary open to
the highest bidder or at the very least
a gun-club psycho with a
secret arsenal in the basement

My earliest piece was a carved Colt 45
made to fit snugly into my
red leather cowboy holster
once, my sister entered a competition
on my behalf that won me a battery
driven machine gun to go along with
the tin ARP warden's hat I found at
the tip and painted in camouflage
colours to wear for street games.

Over the years there were various bows
and arrows including a home-made crossbow
of lethal power for playing William Tell
and an axe bought from Woolworths with a
skull and cross-bones burned onto the
handle with a red-hot poker
I stuffed it into my belt whilst
marauding the woods for bonfire material.
there was a bamboo spear made with
a six-inch nail flattened to a blade
by placing it on the railway line

... and enough knives to maintain the
steel industry in Sheffield

By teens, all weapons appalled me,
and now I hate even video games
that glorify the casual blasting of
almost anyone into smithereens

knife-crime scares me to death

Cracks

The best thing about winter was the frozen pond
Near the field at the end of our road
Our parents told us that nobody was to attempt
To walk on the surface under which a world of life
Was miraculously carrying on.
But we ignored them as we slid having run through crisp,
    rime-laden
Grass to leap onto the surface and see how far we could go.

Occasionally cracks would appear.
Mishaps took place, but nobody drowned.
The pond wasn't deep.
Wet trousers and numbed fingers unable to
Undo a shoelace or unbutton a duffle coat was
A perfectly acceptable price to pay for such fun.

We're still not very good at listening.

We stumble across our riven land ignoring
Our children who seem wiser than we ever were.

Night walking

We seldom walk in blackness without the
Glare of artificial light.
Our eyes, so used to phone and screen
To ever brighter cityscapes
Need darkness now and then.

An hour in the dark without recourse
To torch or lamp unearths nuances, shapes
That we can see as eyes adjust, revealing
Substance within opacity.

Our ancestors experienced the dark
Before the all-pervading flood of neon-blue
And sodium white that perpetually glow,
Visible like a bright rash from space at night.

Once I hiked in rural Brittany at night
With fellow scouts to reach a map reference.
What seemed impenetrable became shades
Of charcoal, deft peripheral movements
Picked up by sharpened senses
Made us silent, but alive to more
Than we had thought imaginable.

The dawn found us by a solitary dairy
Wondering if it was acceptable to
Take cartons of milk from the stacked crates
To slake our thirst.

Gigtastic with Michael

Beatlemania not for us
Liked the music not the fuss
What was out and what was in
We liked Dylan and McGuinn
Country Joe and Loving Spoonful
Clever words and very tuneful

Eighteen years and without fear
Wearing army surplus gear
Ferryboat to Liverpool
Levis on and looking cool
John Moore's Uni student gig
Who the fuck are Blodwyn Pig
Alvin Lee and Ten Years After
Getting pissed collapse in laughter
America played by The Nice
Worth it all at twice the price
Burning flags and raging crowd
Ear-drums aching much too loud

Midnight thumbing for a ride
Cross the Mersey to our side
Walking home with aching feet
Heads still thumping with the beat
Bollocking from mum and dad
Best night that we'd ever had

Mind the gap

To delay the inevitable
induction into the adult
workforce we chose deferred
PGCE courses didn't even want to
be teachers bugger that for a game
of soldiers and while we're at it
bugger the armed forces too
with their tendency to hoover
up Northern working class lads
with promises to see the world
we chose our own way setting out
with army surplus rucksacks and
about fifty quid each to conquer
Europe slightly dodgy metaphor
given the relative proximity of
wartime memories but unlike
our fathers we had peace love and
all that stuff rather than you know
actual tanks and rifles

ferry to Ostend and then stuck out
our thumbs and hoped for the
kindness of strangers which as it
turned out was evident to quite
some degree okay so older French
types would give us two fingers
and shout stuff about cheveux longs
thank god for a grammar school
education eh but younger types
were keen to give us a lift so they

could practice their English
you are from Liverpool do you know
Les Beatles bien sure we'd say
they all lived on our street and in
fact we're only here because we're
taking a break from our band
before we launch into a career
as the next big thing from
Merseyside aren't we Robbo

in Italy a smiling chap gave us a lift
in an impossibly small Fiat and with
halting English demanded to know
what our fathers had done in the war
turned out he hated Il Duce which was
just as well since my dad had been
at Monte Cassino where he was injured
by misdirected American ordnance
our new Italian amigo insisted
on buying us lunch what the fuck are
olives we mouthed at each other but
free food is free food when you have
little cash and no chance of messaging
mummy and daddy to simply send
more money by the Pony Express to the
British embassy in whereversville
at Brindisi we slept on a marble floor
waitng for the boat to Greece at 6.00am
a kind cleaning lady mopped the space
around us without asking us to move

and then brought us tiny cups of
strong bitter coffee somewhat
unlike Maxwell House or Camp
Coffee the wartime chicory essence
substitute for the real thing
on Corfu we met Rick an American
draft dodger we played Greek
monopoly while it rained for three
days and discovered the beneficial
effects of ouzo and Seven Up
in Athens we sold half a litre of
blood in order to have just about
enough money to get home having tried
to persuade the lovely Greek nurse to take
a litre so that we could maybe eat more
than just bread and tomatoes on the way back
it wasn't what is now called a gap-year it was
a two month hiatus before reality set in
on our return I discovered that
my dad had got cancer after a lifetime
devoted to Woodbines and I just got my
first teaching job before he died safe
in the knowledge that his son had
hauled himself up into the lower
echelons of the middle classes
showing that social mobility had
some credibility in those days
as long as you minded the gap

Having an ice-cream at Parkgate

A solitary gull dissects the sky,
And ghostly Wales is faint in filigree.
The sandstone quay worn low, the marsh-grass high,
The stately Dee moves slowly out to sea.

Imagine Cromwell's army in its might,
By dawn's light on the misty sea,
The course set sail to Ireland for a fight,
To force rebellious Catholics to their knees.

And now there simply are no ships in sight,
The estuary lies strangled in the mud
The birds now own the wind by right,
And history is buried now for good.

Along the quay with ice-cream cone in hands,
The people walk and do not understand.

The naming of rooms

My mum's house was the last one on her road to have a
    washhouse,
Where a chipped Belfast sink, sat next to an ancient Hotpoint that
    had replaced the dolly-tub and mangle several lifetimes ago.

Grandma, who lived with us, referred to 'the scullery' and 'the
    pantry' in which
A glassless window-grill kept food fresh in the days before
    fridges.

Kitchenettes were cutting edge and the parlour was where
Visitors of sufficient importance drank tea from the best china.

Later, the front room was where we huddled on the three-piece
Around the coal-fire watching Wilfred Pickles while our backs
Were freezing in winter.
The box-room, where I slept, too small for a full bed, had a
    home-made
Bed-frame screwed to the walls.
There was ice on the inside of the windows on cold mornings
    when I
woke. The fog-horn across the River Mersey heralded the dawn.

Now I live an open-plan life with space and flexibility to
    accommodate my
Habitat fuelled wishes.

Upstairs there is a study and en-suite bathrooms to stimulate
the estate-agent's
Purple prose ... should we decide to sell, upgrade, downsize,
relocate or
Otherwise fulfil our lofty ambitions (yes, we have a loft
conversion).

The block-paved front removes the need to tend or weed or
watch the
Slow, but spectacular emergence of spring flowers.

Arresting development

why do school drama productions appear to
rely so often on American musicals and Andrew
Lloyd doodah and his mate's outmoded bollocks?
Richard and Mick had sixty plus eager inner-city
kids, mostly girls wildly committed to drama so
they wrote their own script about the
suffragettes called 'Sisters' and why not, Manchester
where we were was also where the Pankhursts
got their shit together so like, let's do it

one successful school run to adoring parents
and doubting but amazed staff (what do these
young, leftie teachers think they're doing, in my
day ... blah, blah, blah ...) and one end of show
drunken celebration (we told you they were
irresponsible) later and we decided to go to
the Edinburgh Festival that summer of 1979
with a cast of thousands to put on our play
to the world at The Fringe

thank god health and safety was a dull twinkle
in someone's eyes rather stark reality
we'd never have done it otherwise
so, 70+ kids 12-18 one church community
centre living in the basement
play performed upstairs
a minibus load of costumes and props
a licence to perform and there we were

we'd raided the school canteen and taken
giant pots and pans, kids divided into
dorms (how Mallory Towers) to prevent
teenage pregnancies and we had cooking rotas
and cleaning teams, Christ, half this lot from
Gorton were ideal armed services cannon
fodder so maybe we were just setting them
off on the right path, but without the marching
and rifles ... plenty of sergeant major like
shouting though at rehearsals, ' you haven't
learned your lines, you 'orrible ...'

who would come to see us we thought,
so we did a publicity stunt in the centre
of Edinburgh and Dave Jones, in his suffragette
arresting policeman's outfit got arrested for
by a real copper for getting carried away
directing the traffic as it happened
he was carried away to the local nick
I had to plead with the desk sergeant
for Dave's release, after much grovelling,
'I promise I'll never do a play about the Suffragettes again',
so that he could perform in that evening's show
a coach-load of American school kids came to see us
some early feminists were blown away and The
Scotsman reviewed our play and loved it

we put a disco on every night until the early hours
to stop our little dears wandering out
into the less salubrious areas of
the city where our venue was located
the church minister loved us and
what we were doing

two kids became drama teachers
and playwrights one joined Corrie as a stalwart
for years and Mick became a full-time successful
writer for Radio TV and huge community
projects but the best was that Dave married Julie (eventually)
and became the most successful theatre in education
group in the North with plays written by Mick
perfomed to this day for thousands of kids

what a festival it was, never been more
stressed knackered or proud

There's something about starry winter nights

Get away from the neon urban glare on a cloudless night and
    the sky
Reveals itself.
Stars are pinpricks in lush, blue velvet, in numbers beyond
Our imagination.
They flicker and fizz like synapses across
An infinite brain.

Why is it that I feel more alive, more connected on such nights?
Perhaps my DNA reaches back through millennia to
Ancient northern ancestors, wood fires lit against the cold,
Staring skywards in the same wonder as I feel now.

Today's planet would shock them more than a shooting star's
    flight
Across the icy, still air, but the night sky,
Would be so infinitesimally different as to be almost
The same.

There's something about starry winter nights …

Raise your eyes to the horizon

If you raise your eyes in the city you might
Just catch the sun sinking to the west
Before dusk, reflecting off high-rise windows.
Victorian buildings reveal their true identity
Often carved in stone below the eaves,
But above the garish modern, neon frontage
Of a department store or eatery.

On Werneth Low look eastwards towards
Silhouettes of hill and peak in shades of
Green or khaki and sometimes the mauves
And lilacs of heather interrupted by the
Burnt patches of summer fires,
More frequent now under the earth's
Warming climate.

An upraised head releases the neck's tensions,
Balances our weighty skulls and helps us
To scan the distant horizon for glimpses
Of a wider world beyond our shortsightedness.

Enough

Charlie the Basset needed a walk so
we stood on the step that
Christmas Day locking the door
dog-lead straining and
an excited Emily, all of two and
a half years old clutching a small
plastic shopping bag, a drum and a
rubber washable dog for bath-time.

A quick snap of the camera immortalised
the joy of these bedside presents
which she thought more than enough
to satisfy her expectation.

Little did she know the mass of toys to
come later that day from doting parents,
aunties and grandparents that would overwhelm
her into a grumpy hyper-happiness of excess.

What constitutes enough … love, support, worry,
help, advice, guidance, boundaries, interference?

Do we fall short, overload or stumble towards
some way we deceive ourselves into
thinking that works?
Larkin says we fuck them up which may
be true but difficult to swallow.

Retrospect is great and tends to paper over
much that happened long ago.

Maybe a third generation will give a chance
to learn from the past and occasionally
get it right through the experience of a
lifetime of improvisation and guesswork.

Family Tree

The copper beech in our front garden is laden with metaphor,
Spring buds slowly repeating their annual miracle of unfolding,
Gloriously green in summer ripening nuts crunching
Underfoot on the drive or lodged into shoe soles,
Shedding misshapen pennies in autumn
And skeleton-bare in winter, stark
Against a moonlit night sky.

The raising of morning blinds reveals a
Window-framed sculpture, sometimes with
Squirrels scuttling around its muscled torso
Driving the dog insane,
Sometimes fat pigeons casually precision bomb my car
With droppings the colour of seasonal fruit.

The smell of wood-burning stoves is my reminder
That November is the month of leaf-sweeping
The rhythmic swish of broom drowned out by
The noise of morning traffic.

Walking the dog

Solitary men are legitimised when walking a dog
what would sometimes be a suspicious glance from a
stranger turns to smiles because of the simple
presence of a needy, vulnerable canine.

In Philip Pullman's stories, characters are shadowed
by animal daemons, their souls in appropriate forms
like slavering wolves for baddies or a playful lemur for a goodie.
I'll settle for Nellie the cockapoo, her blond quiff
turning the clock back fifty years to a slimmer, fitter, less bald
version of me.

She follows, she leads, she weaves her way between trees
investigates smells and sounds reporting back in her doggy way
never quite letting me out of sight, invisibly roped by ties of
    affection
and need, giving vicarious pleasure to anybody who she
    encounters.

Walking the dog, feeding the spirit ... it's all the same.

Mindfulness

What if loss of memory was just
A bloated mind too full of information like
A smart-phone past its gigabyte limit?

Perhaps we could select which memories to
Keep and which to consign to the trash-can like unwanted emails
It might prove to be a difficult exercise.

Save the disastrous seventh birthday party or the awkward first
kiss?
The day we won the cup or the '97 election?
The personal or the universal?

Leave space for forthcoming joys
Or assume that anything of significance
Has already happened?

As each new, unfolding event occurs, decide whether to
Jettison an existing memory in order to make way for the new
The balance of past, present and possible future

Held together in a second before the inevitable loss
Of something that was, is or could be worth keeping.
Might it be that we have more than the moment to consider?

Living in Myopia

Hunter-gatherers scanned the distance across endless grasslands
in search of their next meal, aware of
the desperate claws of their own predators
patiently waiting.

We, on the other hand, rarely look beyond the immediate
the smartphone, the monitor, the headline,
the next meal, the next meeting, the next fulfillment
of desire.

Our eyes and minds accustomed to the short distance,
high-rise blocking horizons of possibility
aching necks and straining eyes permanently tense
too seldom lengthening to seek out distance
afraid to look too far ahead for fear of what we might find.

Tools (for Will)

Stanley plane and tenon saw
Neatly mounted on the wall.
Bit and brace to pierce wood
Worn with age, but still as good
As when it sat in older hands
At a time and in a land
That's long since gone, but valued still
By those who yet possess the will
To make and mend to carve and cut,
To plan and measure, not discard,
To build by hand, it's not too hard,
With time and patience borne in mind
Perhaps it's possible to find
Some continuity at last
Re-cycled from a worthwhile past.

New landscape

But isn't it very cold in Iceland? I said
Yes, but we'll be walking and exploring
All day so we'll get warm
We'll get the right gear. Haz likes gear
And so we flew northwards, very northwards
Male bonding, father-son relationship enhancing
Break to get fit and hang out in snow
We were entering a new landscape

The 4-wheel drive took us to a high
Moon-scaped plateau of impossible
Beauty and wild dreadful threat
The wind nearly ripped off the doors
As we left the car to stagger a short way
Into the icy wastes black moulded rocks
Peeking out here and there from the whiteness

Afterwards we found the secret lagoon
And swam outdoors while snowflakes
Feathered our faces and arms as the
Rest of our bodies warmed in the
Sulphurous soup that surrounded us

Pastel coloured houses in Reykjvik
Open air mythological sculptures
Impossibly expensive beer and decent food
At five-star prices were our daily rewards
For hikes along black sand beaches and
Twisting jagged valleys
Wind slowing our pace to a stagger
And a memorable journey behind a snow-plough
On the way to see steaming cateracts and
Spouting geysers that defied gravity

We didn't fall out
We slept like tired logs
We cooked for each other
... maybe I did most of it
And emerged again intact into our
Old, but slightly altered landscape

How did I ever find the time ...

If yet another retired person says to me
'I'm busier now than when
I was working ...'
I shall very probably imagine punching them
On the nose (a get-out clause for pacifists)

Either these people had a bloody easy job
Or they are utterly deceiving themselves.

You cannot compare chalk with cheese
Or bacon butties with any vegan alternative
To the breakfast barm.

Answering the question, 'What do you do?'
Past a certain age, can be problematic.
Do you quickly shift to vicarious mode where
Children and grandchildren define your life?

Does a list of age-appropriate hobbies
Constitute a suitable answer?
Can the word 'cruise' be mentioned at all?

How about, 'I rage at the dying of the light!'
'I write erotic poetry for my many lovers.'
'I daub anti-austerity graffiti on the viaduct walls
For the benefit of passing commuters in the hope
Of raising their political awareness.'

Or perhaps you just say, 'I write shit poetry.'

Ways

Our lives are made of ways, be they footpaths through
Leafy tunnels of speckled summer sun or
Clogged motorway ring-roads round high-rise cities that
Pierce the murk towards the
Autumn evening sky.

Each route we travel ignores those not taken
Other lives not lived, people not encountered,
Such realms of possibility that if dwelt upon
Lead to regret and disappointment.

There is no sacred parchment map or GPS
To lead us to our next direction.
Such notions are the stuff of insecure imagination
Fed to us to sustain the myths of religion.

Like the shark we must keep moving
Through whatever ocean we are in.

A Bitter-Sweet Story

We love sleep but hate death,
Love to spend, but hate debt.

Horror films entertain us
But we can't take brutal reality.

We long to be slim as we crave
 The sugar-rush of chocolate.

We despise the rich,
Then buy lottery tickets in hope of joining them.

We deplore poverty wages,
Whilst queuing to buy sweatshop clothes.

We desert our gods,
Yet search for the spiritual to fill our emptiness.

We journey by jet,
In search of the melting ice-cap.

We are critical of others,
Yet our own skins are thin as silk.

We aspire to celebrity,
But demand our right to privacy.

We want the earth because we think we deserve it,
Whilst we meekly watch it choke and burn.

We are hedonists struggling with conscience,
Drinkers who wish to be sober,
Stay-at-home explorers,
Caring psychopaths,
Compassionate torturers,
Hopefully despairing.

Are we just oxy-morons?

Seating Arrangements

February, Manchester 2017: leaden skies and the threat of rain.
A re-creation of The Last Supper is being set up. Seating
arrangements are in hand to get the picture right.
No painting on a wall.
No 15th Century Italian Convent, but a carefully planned digital
snap in a church community hall in Miles Platting.

Of course, the vicar will be Jesus, reaching for bread and wine,
or an approximation thereof – in this case Warburton's white-
sliced, extra thick and some strong tea, which is the life-blood
of this community.

Day-Centre stalwarts and regulars are the apostles, eager to
know who will betray their master, aghast at the news of his
impending departure.

I suspect that none of them ever betrayed anyone. Their faces
betray only lives lived, loves won and lost, jobs won and lost,
kids raised and flown the nest, hardships endured.

These apostles are mostly women, backbone of their
community, always there to help and comfort, grafting for
others: Jesus would have approved.

They hold their poses for as long as it takes, unsmilingly as the
photographer wants them, taking it seriously, waiting for the
moment when it's done and dusted and they can relax.

The backdrop, a stage full of camp-beds and bedding for the homeless: Jesus would have approved all right, might even have changed the course of history had his final meal been tea and toast in North Manchester.

Not sure it would have been called supper though ...

Might have been dinner or tea, not lunch – we don't do lunch here.
Perhaps if the meal was mid-morning, it could have been The Last Brunch ... perhaps not.

Salvador Dali, Andy Warhol (with celebrities) both tried The Last Supper. Vik Muniz, whoever he is/was, did it in chocolate syrup.

This is better. Real people, real lives.

To see the original, you have to apply in writing months beforehand.
This photograph will be up on the community hall wall for all and sundry to look at anytime they like.

The Southbank

Beach huts built on artificial sands,
The colours not yet bleached by summer sun.
But Father Thames cannot quite understand,
Some trendy London artists having fun.

Above it all a futuristic view,
The lowering, high-rise silhouette at night,
Such pristine gleaming towers for the few,
Erected for the rich without a fight.

The cardboard beds beneath the London Eye,
Unseen from lofty penthouse roofs,
Though restless sleepers cannot reason why,
And therein lies the cold, uneasy truth.

The river will run dry before the world is fair,
Hypocracy and greed sit safely in their lair.

Montaigne's Cat

Michel de Montaigne invented
the essay in the 16th Century
in his tower near Bergerac
I don't think he imagined the
sense of dread that his invention
would introduce into the lives
of future students but I'm sure
that had he known it the thought
would have amused him

he wrote about:
emotions
breaking wind
how to die
prognostication
how we weep
how we laugh
solitude
drunkenness

few topics escaped his interest

he looked inwards not outwards
making the study of himself his
life's work and yet not in an
arrogant or egotistical way
nobody had done that before

one day whilst writing he noticed
his cat was reacting to the sound
and movement of his quill and
instead of becoming annoyed at
the potential interruption to
his work he smiled and thought
why cannot my cat regard me
and what I do in the same way
that I or any other human being
might regard her

he realized that the world was not
created simply as the plaything of
people a rather dangerous thought
at the time and that all creatures
had an equal right to look at the world
and be puzzled or amused by the
behaviour of other beings

scratching a bird's feather across
parchment having dipped it in blue
liquid could well appear ridiculous
in the eyes of his cat

who are we to claim that
it is not so

Did Jean-Paul Sartre work out?

On a treadmill at the gym
drink in hand and ear-buds in
podcast on and Nike socks
listening hard to Brian Cox.

Is this how it ought to be
for multitasking you and me?
or maybe there's another way
to get the most out of our day.

Simply walk in open air
look around and see what's there
listen to each tiny sound
feel your feet upon the ground.

Breathe the air and feel the breeze
move yourself but keep your ease
look above to see the sky
vision wide and head held high.

Give attention to each task
is that just too much to ask?
what would Jean-Paul Sartre say
if you lived your life this way?

I would like to learn to listen

Engage eye contact posture in non-intrusive
relaxed mode close mouth turn off phone
dismiss distractions nod encouragingly

allow silences

temper responses with appropriate facial expressions
reflect support and empathy where necessary
people are various some need more space
more stillness more pause to frame
their thoughts

so let them

sounds easy but I'm not entirely there yet
the urge to interrupt to complete the sentence
to offer the obviously fascinating perspective
of my own experience is sometimes too strong
so off I go rambling on about me when I should

simply listen

it's not solely about people
the walk with the dog attended by birdsong
murmering of breeze in trees
aircraft aloft distant traffic rain on roofs

be aware of it all

then the inner voice with all its cunning
sometimes supportive others critical
reflective petty philosophical angry
guilt-ridden joyous anxious
smug embarrassed

and often ignored

is there a balance a still point in the
turning world where self and
not-self might coexist in harmony?

The view from my window

I glance up from reading to see
A pink and grey western sky
Form a glorious backdrop to the
Setting sun over suburban roofs.

I Whatsapp a picture to the family
Spread far and wide this late winter
Afternoon, Lanzarote, Prague, Cadiz
In the dead time between Christmas
And the coming of a new year.

It still seems like a minor miracle
That I should see within the hour
Three more sunsets from afar
Bounced off star-like satellites
To reach me where I sit.

What gifts to receive in return for
The simple act of noticing a sunset.

Roman Walls

How long did soldiers toil,
placing block after chiseled block
of sandstone carefully into each
preordained space?
no two blocks the same shape
the colours ranging from
deep red to pale gold.

Miles from home, under the
beady eye of the engineer
in sheeting rain and wild wind
muscles straining against
ropes and pulleys
to build a statement, a defence
against the hordes.

We meet in an old pub in
Chester, nine school friends,
fifty years on from those shared
teenage years of spots and sport
music and carefree days.

After lists of ailments, ops,
grand-children and modest
amounts of beer, a measured
stroll round the walls between
pubs, I come to appreciate the
pleasure of lives quarried
from the same place shifting
slightly here or there but
grounded in the same earth.

Sic transit memoria

We had always known that a family gravestone
existed on the maternal side somewhere in Blackpool
near where we were born so Jackie and I headed
to the coast for a day out accompanied by Mum's
ashes in a serviceable plastic urn

we strolled the prom had fish and chips visited
The Winter Garden's faded glory to imagine the
first encounter of Fred and Eileen on the massive
dance-floor jitterbugging to a raucous big band
I could see floral frocks and double-breasted suits
with massive flies and pleated wide legs
youthful joy not even as old as our own children

off a windy central pier we deposited a
handful of ashes each into the brown sea
taking care to judge the wind not really wanting
to snort a faceful of our own DNA

we tracked down the cemetery clutching
an old photograph taken in 1967 after Grandma's
name was added to the stone and a bill for
said engraving with the plot number attached

arriving at the spot we found nothing
no family stone no timeless memorial
to our past just uneven turf and emptiness
look on my works, ye mighty and whatever

we looked around and became aware of
numerous teetering gravestones fallen
monuments some even half protruding
from the soil like sunken wrecks

the thin sandy soil had swallowed up our story
gradually allowing the heavy stone of our
family history to be absorbed back into
the earth from whence it came

David, listen to some jazz, man

Blow some bubbles, baby, let it all hang out.
Be a sixty year old dude and learn to sing and shout.
Start to play the saxophone, walk the Pennine Way,
Photograph New York at Dawn. Come on! Learn to play!

Cut your pin-stripe suit to shreds, ditch the mobile phone.
Tell Whitehall to, 'Go screw yourself! I want to be alone.'
Plant your garden, grow your mind, read philosophy,
Take up yoga, stretch that back maybe you will see,

That possibilities abound for you, if you free your mind.
So, take those East End roots of yours, seek and ye shall find ...
Whatever's really out there, man, just grab it by the throat,
And shake it, bake it, but don't fake it, make it float your boat.

I love you, dude, but loosen up before you get too old.
There's more to life than meets the eye, so come on, break your
mould.
Oh, Lord, give us temptation and forget our daily bread,
We want Brewdog IPA, before we wind up dead.

When we're all together, dude, with our free bus-pass,
Let's set the geriatric world on fire. Let's kick some teenage ass.
So, swim in wild waters, nude, dude, in moats and streams and
seas,
And banish crown-green bowling, man, for all eternity.

Let's not go gentle as we age, let's revolutionise
And view the world for what it is, before our very eyes.
You get the message? Get the drift? And your gorgeous wife,
 You make the most of every day, make sure to live your life.

The Canny Lad of Darlington * *

This is an additional character from "The Tales" until
recently unknown.

He were a bonny swain who oft liked to relax
In leisure-wear he bought from T.K. Maxx.
Fair Julia, his wife, was loth to let him go,
But pilgrims hear a higher voice and so
Without a second thought or pause,
He set off in some walking togs from Go Outdoors.

At night the other pilgrims tossed and turned, but could not
    sleep
While P.E. Steve (as he was known) would fall right off
    without a peep . . .
. . . save for a snorting snore of power so renown
The like of which was nowhere to be found.

When came his turn to tell his tale to other pilgrims there,
He told of his adventures on the water, land and air.
His skiing feats left pilgrims' mouths agape,
And when he told of swimming in an icy lake
They marvelled at his wholesome, northern grit . . .
. . . of course they really only knew the half of it.

Of Striding Edge, he told, how scrambling in the snow
He saw the deadly frozen depths below
With his three doughty pals in tow
Without a single gaiter nor a walking pole
They conquered Lakeland's fearsome peak
(Though Mart stopped more than once to take a leak.)

To show his softer side'
Steve told of driftwood artworks conjured from his lively mind,
And made those fellow pilgrims each
A keepsake carved from wood that he could find

He told of magic flights by air to witness far exotic sights
Beyond the dreams of Canterbury's lights.
His fellow pilgrims couldn't understand
Steve's picture of this oriental land .
He made them see the ancient stones of Angkor Wat
And see the grandeur of this holy spot.

And when they asked his age, 'twas 60 to the day
The Wife of Bath stood up with this to say,
"I swear to you by yonder shining star,
Steve Hewie is the best man here by far!"

Mortal Tears

Age brings a tendency to more frequent tears
A snatch from a song, an old photograph,
A glimpse of grainy, monochrome footage
From some bygone age seem to trigger
Something more deeply felt.
Unravellling the tissue layers
Reveals a common thread
Of mortality, the sharp awareness of a
Younger self who no longer exists
Nor will ever again hear that same
Song lyric for the first time
Or be snapped in that
Youthful, carefree pose on that
Day with those people, in that sunlight.

The past has no monopoly on significance
But the present tends ever more towards
A vicariousness of experienced lived
Through those who came after and will
In turn become what we are now.

CV 19

Lock down
Wise up
Stay in
Chill out
Check in
Help out
Calm down
Stock up
Near to
Far from
Press up
Hang on
Stand by
Look at
Safe to
Spread out
Keep off
Switch on
Make do
Just don't
Can't stand
So won't
Be as
Live like
Walk there
Ride bike
Short stroll
Long hike
Cover up
Wash down

Hope to
Dream of
When will
Don't know
Be still
It's just
What's fair
Too much
Don't care
Life will
Some time
Be . . .

Now we are 70

Jumpers for goalposts and lampposts for wickets,
Sweltering summers of tennis and cricket.
Brown leather sandals with T-shirts and shorts,
Endless obsessions with hobbies and sports.

National Health glasses and teeth full of fillings,
Obsolete money like pounds, pence and shillings.
Was that how it was in that faraway past,
In that monochrome world that we all thought would last?

Then along came The Beatles, The Stones and The Byrds,
And Bob Dylan's songs with such powerful words.
When Levis and Wranglers became all the rage,
And all teens together broke out of their cage.

When Wembley itself was our Mecca of choice,
The football sublime and the crowd in good voice.
When Hurst scored a hat-trick and Peters scored too,
And we beat the Germans by four goals to two.

Best days of our life viewed through rose-tinted specs?
Or an over-hyped myth minus booze, drugs and sex?
So, as 'three score and ten' has arrived here at last,
Let's just look to the future and not dwell on the past.

Lightning Source UK Ltd.
Milton Keynes UK
UKHW011839050820
367752UK00001B/75